Big Daddy's Joke Book

D1351769

Also in Armada:

Big Daddy's Joke Book

with cartoons by Graham Round

An Armada Original

Big Daddy's Joke Book was first published in the
U.K. in 1981 in Armada by Fontana Paperbacks, 14
St. James's Place, London SW1A 1PS.

The arrangement of this collection is copyright
© Bill Howard 1981

© Illustrations Armada 1981

Printed and bound by The Anchor Press, Tiptree,
Essex.

Big Daddy first started his career as a professional wrestler 18 years ago, and is now one of the most famous and popular fighters in the ring. In 1980, when Armada carried out a survey of schoolchildren all over the country to find out who were their top 200 favourite personalities – Big Daddy was No. 1! His wrestling matches are often seen on television, and he has appeared on "Jim'll Fix It" and other celebrity programmes. Big Daddy's real name is Shirley Crabtree (not an unusual name for a boy in the part of Yorkshire from which he comes), and he lives in Yorkshire with his wife and daughter.

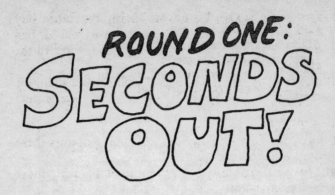

ROUND ONE: SECONDS OUT!

BARBER (To customer): I'm afraid that you've got atomic hair.
CUSTOMER: What on earth is atomic hair?
BARBER: It's suffering from fall-out.

MARY: Ernie's in the removal business now.
ELSIE: Oh ... what's the removal firm?
MARY: It's the local disco. He's their new bouncer.

FIRST HUSBAND: Is your wife very keen on cooking?
SECOND HUSBAND: Not very. Last time we had some friends in for a meal she gave them luncheon vouchers.

WAITER: Perhaps you would like to finish up with a brandy and a cigar, sir?
DISSATISFIED CUSTOMER: No thanks. I don't like to smoke on an empty stomach.

FIRST SCOTSMAN: I saw McTavish the other day walking on crutches. He must have had a bad accident because he could hardly put his feet to the ground.

SECOND SCOTSMAN: Oh, he's all right. He's walking on crutches because his shoes are beginning to wear out.

FIRST CUSTOMER: You don't get many potatoes these days with your fried fish.

SECOND CUSTOMER: No – they must be using those new micro chips.

PATIENT: I feel half dead.

DOCTOR: In that case I'll make arrangements for you to be buried up to the waist.

CUSTOMER: I'm sorry but I've had an accident with this salad.

WAITER: What's the trouble, sir?

CUSTOMER: My knife slipped, and I unfortunately cut this caterpillar in half.

JUDGE: Before I sentence you to be hanged, have you anything to say?

PRISONER: Yes, your honour. I feel absolutely choked.

VAMPIRE WIFE: Dracula, dear, as we are going on holiday tomorrow, remind me to tell the blood man to stop leaving the daily pinta.

Why did the bee go to the bank?
Because it wanted some 'oney.

Why did the cat go to the fridge?
Because it wanted some 'ice.

NEIGHBOUR: I think your dog is feeling uncomfortable.
DOG OWNER: What makes you think that?
NEIGHBOUR: Because he has just leaked the information.

Which was the largest moth ever known?
The mam-moth.

RON: How many languages do you know?
BILL: Three . . . English and French.
RON: What's the third one then?
BILL: Just bad.

ENQUIRER: Are you a turf accountant?
BOOKIE: That's right. Do you want to place a bet?
ENQUIRER: No. I want to know how much grass I'll need to make a tennis court.

FIRST SHOPPER (In cannibal supermarket): How's your husband?
SECOND SHOPPER: Moaning as usual about his health. By the way he goes on you'd think he already had one foot in the gravy.

Mrs. Jones, recently widowed, went to a seance and asked the medium if it would be possible to get in touch with her late husband.

"But of course," said the medium.

"Oh good," replied Mrs. Jones. "That's a relief. I want to know where he put the back door key, because it's missing from under the mat."

FIRST LADY MOTORIST: Do you use your mirror very much when you drive?
SECOND LADY MOTORIST: Heavens no! I make sure my face is properly made up before I start.

FIRST GHOST: I don't know about you, but I don't seem to frighten people any more.

SECOND GHOST: No, we might as well as be dead for all they care.

FIRST WOMAN: My husband wants me to get him something electrical for his birthday present.

SECOND WOMAN: How about an electric chair?

FIRST INDIAN: We don't seem to get any smoke signals from Sitting Bull these days.

SECOND INDIAN: I'm not surprised. He's given up his old fire and gone in for central heating.

Two fat men ran in a race. One ran in short bursts, the other in burst shorts.

At a recent nudist whist drive the booby prize was a clothes brush.

CUSTOMER: Did you say your prices were frozen?
SHOP-KEEPER: Yes sir.
CUSTOMER: That explains why they are so stiff.

MOTHER: Why don't you go out and play football with your little brother?
SON: He doesn't like it, Mum, and I'd much sooner have a real football to kick.

Why are drinkers like parachutists?
Because they don't mind having a drop.

What made the bed spread?
When it saw the pillow slip.

What might happen if you drank too much cider?
You might get apple-plexy (apoplexy).

When is a tennis player like a good preacher?
When he gives a good service.

FIRST BOY: My Dad threatens me with the strap when I
   play up.
SECOND BOY: Does he ever use it?
FIRST BOY: No ... When he takes his belt off to hit me
   his trousers fall down.

What happens when fat people get on the bathroom scales?
They get shown up in a big weigh.

What soldiers are like nudists?
Those that have bearskins (bare skins).

What's the difference between a fierce dog being stroked by a stranger and a bullfighter?
One bites the fool. The other fights the bull.

What's the difference between a bee and a flea?
The bee makes a flight. The flea makes a bite.

Why is the weathercock conceited?
Because he is a vane (vain) creature.

THS WIND IS RUINING MY COMB!

FARMER: I can guarantee that all my eggs are new-laid.
CUSTOMER: How so?
FARMER: Because I've never seen a hen lay an old one.

FIRST MAN: Is your wife a good pastry cook?
SECOND MAN: I should say so. Every time I think of her pastry a lump comes into my throat.

HUSBAND: That steak you gave me last night was terrible. I hope you've got something tonight I can get my teeth into.
WIFE: Yes I have — a glass of water. Take them out and put 'em in that!

What sort of pets are favourites for tea-time?
Crumpets.

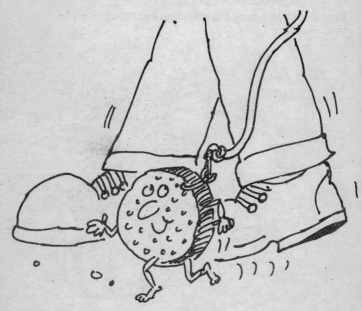

FIRST MAN: Does your wife make good toast?
SECOND MAN: I'm afraid that's a burning question.

EMPLOYMENT OFFICER: I can offer you a job where you will make plenty of good contacts.
APPLICANT: Splendid. What job is that?
EMPLOYMENT OFFICER: Sparring partner to the local boxing champion.

What's the difference between a squeaking hinge and eggs for breakfast?
One begs to be oiled, the other's eggs to be boiled.

How do bluebottles get from one place to another?
On fly-wheels.

What open boat can be filled to the top but will never sink?
A gravy boat.

GIRL (To yacht skipper): And what happens when you have to contend with a lot of wind?
SKIPPER: I usually put my hand over my mouth and say 'pardon'.

Why is a railway terminus a dangerous place?
Because it is a main lion (line) station.

What sort of meat do idiots like?
Chump chops.

What animals can you see in Fleet Street?
The gnus (news).

WAXWORKS GUIDE: Here we have the figure of Wyatt Earp. A most famous Marshall, and a deadly shot.

AMERICAN TOURIST: I knew of someone who drew a gun on him and lived!

MUSEUM GUIDE: And who was that, pray?

AMERICAN TOURIST The local tattooist.

Did you hear about the man who worked in a loony bin? The people he met were just crazy about him.

What did the whisky say when water was poured in his glass?
I'm diluted to meet you.

Why are eggs like bricks?
Because in order to be used they have to be laid.

BIG DADDY'S CORNER

Why do wrestlers remind you of jewellers?
Because they both know a lot about rings.

Why do Big Daddy's opponents remind you of an ice cream cornet?
Because they both get licked.

What happens when Big Daddy's opponents get cold feet?
He gives them socks.

When is Big Daddy like a barber?
When he uses the "scissors".

What do you get if you cross a football defender and a large wave?
A back breaker.

ROUND TWO:
GRUNTS AND GROANS

DENTIST (to patient): I haven't seen you for a very long time.
PATIENT: That's true, but now I'm simply aching to see you again.

FIRST HOUSEWIFE: I must say my husband's taking the "Save Energy" campaign very seriously.
SECOND HOUSEWIFE: Oh? What's he doing about it then?
FIRST HOUSEWIFE: He's stopped working.

FIRST WIFE: My husband's new job is very demanding.
SECOND WIFE: What is it?
FIRST WIFE: He's just become an Income Tax Collector.

MILLIE: My boyfriend has just realised his burning ambition.
MOLLY: And what's that?
MILLIE: He's joined the fire brigade.

What was the name of the famous Jewish detective?
Shylock Holmes.

A gardener has discovered a method of making his tomatoes go red. He just keeps saying rude things to them until they blush.

RUDI: Gerald's taking a sandwich course.
TRUDI: What on earth for?
RUDI: To help him earn his bread and butter, I suppose.

ASTRONAUT (To Ground Control): We're slowing down.
GROUND CONTROL: What's the matter?
ASTRONAUT: We've just been thumbed down by an angel who wants a lift.

What's the best way to get rid of an obstinate tooth?
Use gum powder.

Why is a very fat man like a successful cattle rancher?
Because they both have big spreads.

FIRST MAN: I'm going to take my wife to the seaside
for a change.
SECOND MAN: That's interesting. What are you going
to change her for?

JAN: Molly tells me she's now a director in the film business!
NAN: Quite true. She's an usherette, and directs people to their seats in the local cinema.

When is a piece of wood like a trawling net?
When it's full of knots.

DOCTOR (To clergyman patient): And have you been taking your medicine three times a day as I ordered?
CLERGYMAN: Naturally Doctor. I've obeyed your instructions religiously.

PERCY: D'you know – I've spent years in the saddle.
MARY (Impressed): I didn't know you were a horseman.
PERCY: I'm not, I'm a cyclist.

1ST GOAT: Who's that little goat standing over there?
2ND GOAT: That's my kid brother.

The club member was boasting about his ancestors. "Our family tree," he said, "goes back to the time of William the Conqueror."

"That's nothing," said the oldest member sarcastically. "Our family tree goes back to the time we were hanging from its branches."

A customer walked into a restaurant and asked the manager if they did meals to take away.

"Certainly, sir," said the manager. "Any meals you eat here you are allowed to take away . . ."

FIRST SCOTSMAN: I must say that old McTavish knows how to put the drink away.

SECOND SCOTSMAN: Och aye. It's usually in the cupboard as soon as he sees anyone coming.

Jock McTavish decided to save money on his Christmas cards. When he sent one he wished his friends a Merry Christmas for the next ten years.

TEACHER: What is an obtuse angle?

PUPIL: A thick kind of Ancient Briton.

LULU: I must say that Ernie's hair transplant looks the real thing.

MARY: Especially when he dusts his coat collar with powder and calls it dandruff.

When are sheep like ball-point ink?
When they are put in pens.

What do telephone operators like to celebrate?
Hallo'een (Halloween).

What is a Greek cat's favourite food?
Mous-saka.

EDITOR: Did you write about Lord Nelson?
YOUNG REPORTER: Yes, boss.
EDITOR: How much space did you give him?
YOUNG REPORTER: Oh, the usual — a whole long column to himself.

CUSTOMER: Do you make all kinds of men's wear?
TAILOR: Yes, sir, all kinds.
CUSTOMER: I'm not surprised. The prices you charge are enough to make all men swear.

When is a lettuce like a frightened horse?
When it bolts.

NEWS FLASH: Rescued in the nick of time by a helicopter, the captain of a sinking ship said that he and the crew had missed death by a few winches.

When is a guilty person like a firework?
When he gets let off.

TEACHER: What is garlic?
BOY: It's the sort of language Scotsmen speak.

How does a flea get from one place to another?
By 'itch hiking.

FIRST TAILOR: When I take a holiday I like to get away from it all.
SECOND TAILOR: So where do you go?
FIRST TAILOR: To a nudist camp.

TAILOR: So ye'll be wanting another suit, Mr. McTavish?
McTAVISH: Och aye, same as before. Jacket and trousers, and no pockets.

What piece of new kitchen furniture is like a well-tailored man?
A smart dresser.

TEACHER: What is a tailor's dummy?
BOY: Please, miss, it's what the tailor's baby sucks.

FIRST FLEA: You look a bit seedy these days.
SECOND FLEA: Yes, I'm not feeling up to scratch.

FIRST RHINOCEROS: What on earth is that thing over there?
SECOND RHINOCEROS: That's a hippopotamus.
FIRST RHINOCEROS: Fancy having to live with an ugly face like that!

Why is a burnt match like your pocket money at the end of the week?
Because it is spent.

What sort of horse would be useful if your car battery was flat?
A charger.

How would you call up the police in Germany?
*Pick up the 'phone and say "No" three times in German.
(Nein, Nein, Nein.)*

Why don't you get custard in China?
*How would you like to try and eat custard with chop
sticks?*

"I've diagnosed your trouble," said the psychiatrist to
his patient. "You're feeling all screwed up!"

"That's right," said the surprised patient. "How did
you know?"

"Ever since you got here," said the psychiatrist,
"you've ben trying to get into the waste-paper basket."

What's the difference between the outside of a juicy beef joint and a doormat?
One's the fat that goes with the meat. The other's the mat that goes with the feet.

FIRST COMIC: I got a Golden Wedding Anniversary card from my wife last week.

SECOND COMIC: But you've only been married two years, not fifty!

FIRST COMIC: She said she knew that, but it seemed like fifty to her.

The visitors were admiring the talking ability of Mrs. Green's parrot.

"How on earth did it learn to say so many words?" one asked.

"Oh," explained Mrs. Green, "we had it educated at the local Polly-technic."

MARY: I see much more of Tessa than I used to.
JOAN: Yes, she certainly is putting on a lot of weight.

Two critics were discussing the work of a young painter. "I must say," says one, "since he has adopted the modern style of painting his work has improved out of all recognition."

On what kind of road would you find diamonds?
A dual (jewel) carriageway.

Why are butchers like fox-hunters?
Because they both make arrangements for the meet (meat).

JIM: My wife tried on her diamond ring the other day and discovered that she'd lost a stone.

JOHN: My wife tried on her bikini and found she'd gained one!

FIRST SCOTSMAN: I bet that new wife or yours is a good cook.

SECOND SCOTSMAN: I'm nae so sure. Each time I come home tae supper she makes it a Burns night.

The customer called the waiter over and said angrily, "What on earth is this soup? It's the absolute end."

"You're quite right, sir," said the waiter. "It is the absolute end – it's oxtail."

NEIGHBOUR: Do you grow very much in your garden?

SECOND NEIGHBOUR: Not really. I finished growing when I was about sixteen.

What is the longest known insecet?
The centipede, because its body covers a hundred feet.

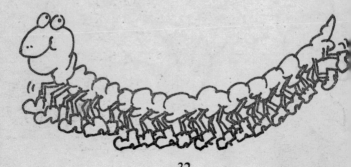

32

Why is it dangerous to read a first-aid book?
Because if you do, you will meet with a chapter of accidents.

Why did knights in armour practise fighting a lot?
To prevent themselves from getting rusty.

While doing a job, a man fell from the top of a ladder. When he got home he told his wife, "Four ribs broken."

"Four ribs broken!" said she. "Which hospital did you go to?

"Didn't have to," said the man. "The four ribs belonged to the man I fell on."

What happened to the chap who accidentally fell into the cement mixer?
He turned out to be a very hard man.

"Did you know," said Molly, "that Peter proposed to me on his bended knees?"

"How old-fashioned and romantic it must have been!" said Polly.

"Not really," said Molly. "His knees were bent because I was sitting on his lap at the time."

TEACHER: Accidents sometimes lead to discoveries which can change the shape of things.
BOY: That's what my Dad discovered when Mum hit a lampost with his car and changed the shape of that.

CUSTOMER: I would like some bits for my dog, please.
BUTCHER: Certainly, madam. What bits are missing?

What did the man do when he switched on the lamp?
He made light of it.

Why is the drum the most popular part of the band?
Because it takes a lot of beating.

BERT: I come from a broken home.
GERT: How did that happen?
BERT: Just after Dad looked for a gas leak with a
    lighted match.

Why did Lady Godiva ride her horse as she did?
Because she had nothing else on at the time.

BIG DADDY'S CORNER

Why is a wrestler like a steeple-chase jockey?
Because they can both get thrown.

Why did the pin-fall?
Because it saw the knee drop.

What's the difference between a big squeeze and a nit?
One's a sort of bear hug. The other's a sort of hair bug.

When is Big Daddy like a bill-poster?
When he gives someone a good pasting.

What's the difference between Big Daddy's hat and a little girl buying sweets?
One's a shiny topper. The other's a tiny shopper.

What two ringside officials represent a very short time?
A couple of seconds.

ROUND THREE:
HEAD BUTTS

What do disc-jockeys wear?
Track suits.

What can run fast yet stay in the same place?
A car engine.

What happened when the cat drank twenty saucers of milk?
It created a lap record.

Why are skyscrapers like joke books?
Because they are full of tall storeys (stories).

Why did Dracula keep his coffin in a vault?
Because it was there he liked to have his vaulty winks (forty winks).

PERCY: Wrestlers remind me of jewellers.
JAMES: Why?
PERCY: Because they both know a lot about rings.

Why is an old car like a sausage?
Because it's a banger.

Why is a road map like a tree?
Because it has routes (roots).

What did one piano say to the other piano?
You may consider yourself grand but at least I'm upright.

What sort of horse is like an old joke?
A chestnut.

Why did the robot go mad?
Because he had a screw loose.

Mr. and Mrs. Jones have decided to open up a butcher's shop. They described it as a joint enterprise.

Why is an honest man like a railway crossing?
Because they are both on the level.

Why is Prince Charles like part of the postal service?
Because he is the Royal male (mail).

Why are slimmers thrifty people?
Because they try to cut down waste (waist).

What happened when the ostrich swallowed the watch?
He found it very time-consuming.

What rises and falls yet stays in the same place?
A barometer.

Why did the horse box?
Because it saw the Suffolk Punch.

What kind of sea-gull can't fly?
A bi-seagull (bicycle).

When is a sailor like a wooden plank?
When he's aboard.

Why did Caesar come to Britain?
Because he liked to be a-roamin (a Roman).

How do chickens communicate?
By using fowl language.

Why did the bald man buy another wig?
Because he felt it would do him good to have a change of 'air.

What gloves can be held but not worn?
Fox-gloves.

What's the difference between a pilot and a stunt flier?
One's an aeronaut, the other's an aero-nut.

Why is petrol like the contents of a ship's hold?
Because it makes the cargo (car go).

What did the artist do when he caught people looking in his window?
Drew the curtain.

WHAT'S THE DIFFERENCE BETWEEN:

A gun slinger and a fog horn?
One shoots from the hip, the other hoots from the ship.

A successful mountain climber and a fat man?
One scales the tops. The other tops the scales.

Someone who has just about enough to do, and a glass
of flat lemonade?
One's fairly busy, the other's barely fizzy.

A policeman and a slimmer?
One pounds the beat, the other beats the pound.

A boxer and somebody with a cold?
*One has to know his blows. The other has to blow his
nose.*

A tug and an ice-berg?
One tows the ship. The other shows the tip.

A person about to have an operation, and someone
labelling a piece of luggage?
One lies on the table. The other ties on the label.

A pint pot and a flea?
One's a beer mug, the other's a mere bug.

The girl who's smart, and the one who decides to do
something?
*One knows how to mind her make-up. The other knows
how to make her mind up.*

POLICE SERGEANT: Is that a true description of your missing mother-in-law?

CALLER: Yes, sergeant.

POLICE SERGEANT: In that case, it's obvious we'd better start by getting in touch with the zoo.

FIRST MAN: What's the best thing you've seen on the telly this week?

SECOND MAN: The switch.

What's a cheerful hippopotamus called?
An happypotomus.

What's a baby hippopotamus called?
An nappy-potamus.

Why is the director of an orchestra like a piece of copper wire?
Because they are both good conductors.

Why is a busy church bell like an old joke?
Because it is always being tolled (told).

What did the musician say on December the twelfth?
There aren't many Chopin days left to Christmas.

What's the difference between a leg-puller and a watch?
One's a micky-taker, the other's a ticky-maker.

What animal answers to a knock?
A dormouse (door mouse).

Why are good allotments like interesting stories?
Because they both have well-laid plots.

Why are boot-blacks clever people?
Because they shine at their work.

What do you get if you cross the middle of a dartboard with someone having forty winks?
A bull-dozer.

Why are astronauts successful people?
Because they always go up in the world.

What did the housewife say to the plumber after he had mended her cistern?
Tanks very much.

What did the keen young plumber call his new-born son?
Lew (loo).

Why is a tap with a faulty washer like the fat from roast beef?
They are both dripping.

Why is a plumber like a Scottish musician?
Because they are both expert with the pipes.

Why is it dangerous for a car to stop?
Because it brakes (breaks).

What do Chinese cannibals eat with?
Chap-sticks.

What do you get if you cross a foppish person with the king of the jungle?
A dandy-lion (dandelion).

Why is a leg of pork like an old radio set?
Because on both of them you get crackling.

What is a philatelist?
A person of the right stamp.

What do you get if you cross a policeman with a telegram?
Copper wire.

What is a string quartet?
Four people playing tennis.

What kind of bowler is like a spider?
A spinner.

What is the difference between a chief cattle drover and a judge?
One is a trail boss. The other is a trial boss.

Why is the corner of the ring like a pillar box?
Because there you will always find the post.

BIG DADDY'S CORNER

What's the difference between Big Daddy and a baker?
One can break the bed, the other can bake the bread.

What does being big and heavy do for Big Daddy?
Makes him a huge success.

If you reach a busy road junction what sort of ring fighter might you think of?
It would be welter-weight (well to wait).

And what sort of ring fighter would you be reminded of if you saw a red traffic signal?
Just a light wait (light weight).

Why is a collector of old iron like a wrestling promoter?
Because he is a scrap dealer.

ROUND FOUR:
BODY SLAMS

PATIENT: I wish you could stop me talking to myself, doctor.

PSYCHIATRIST: Why are you worried about it?

PATIENT: I'm a door-to-door salesman, and I keep persuading myself to buy things I don't really want.

FRIEND: Is it true that when you wake up you always find yourself on the bedroom floor?

PAL: That's right. When I get into bed I always drop off to sleep.

TEACHER: Why were the Pilgrim Fathers called the early settlers?

BOY: Because they always paid their bills promptly.

Why is it hard to get to the top in all-in wrestling?

Because you have a mighty big struggle to get there.

Why is the Lord Mayor like an old-fashioned lavatory cistern?
Because they both have chains hanging from them.

MAISIE: What's a sick joke, Daisy?
DAISY: The sort that you don't bring up in polite society.

CUSTOMER: I'm in a hurry. Can you lay on a plate of ham for me?
WAITER: I'd like to oblige, sir, but I'm too big to get on one.

PATIENT: I'm going bald; what can I do about it?
DOCTOR: Sleep with your windows open. That way you'll get plenty of fresh 'air.

BERT: Your car's making a funny noise.
TOM: Yes, I've just had the engine tuned.
BERT: Ah, I recognise the tune it's playing now – it's "Any Old Iron!"

TEACHER: What is an ikon?
BOY: Please, miss, it's what an oak tree comes from.

CUSTOMER: I'll have a drink for starters.
WAITER: Aperitif, sir?
CUSTOMER: Yes, I'll have a pair of those for the steak to follow.

If a hen drank water with whisky in it what would you get?
Scotch eggs.

FRIEND : How's your wife getting on with her driving lessons?
HUSBAND : I'm not sure, but judging by the state of the car, she must be taking a crash course.

What is the Scottish Barbers' favourite winter sport?
Curling.

What happened when the motorist was told he'd have to take a breath test?
He just blew up.

FIRST BUSINESSMAN: I always go to my bank manager for a loan just before Easter.
SECOND BUSINESSMAN: Why?
FIRST BUSINESSMAN: Because at that time it is always Lent.

Why are fat people often important?
Because they carry a lot of weight.

FIRST VICAR: Do you find that your congregation tends to drop off these days?
SECOND VICAR: Yes. But I don't really mind so long as they don't snore too loudly.

What did the royal elephant get on his birthday?
A twenty-one bun salute.

When is a cat like a fat man's belt?
When it has to be let out.

FAT PATIENT : What are my chances of losing weight,
  doctor?
DOCTOR : Slim.

WIFE : Mr. McTavish has invited us and the neighbours
  in for a drink.
HUSBAND : I wonder which one of us will get it.

What happens to a clock when it is fixed securely to a
wall?
It remains fast.

POLL : Have you seen Mary's new dog?
MOLL ; Yes . . . it's a pedigree.
POLL : How can you tell?
MOLL : Because it barks with such a posh accent.

I SAY..
WOFF...
...WOFF!!

Where can you get sea-food, and raise money at the same time?
At the local prawn shop.

What did the oil sheik say when he left his friends?
Oil see you again.

FIRST HUSBAND : My wife has a very biased outlook.
SECOND HUSBAND : In what way?
FIRST HUSBAND : Usually when we go shopping. It's always bias this, bias that . . .

Why is someone checking his football results like an orchestra?
Because they both read their scores.

MARY : When you work, are you covered by insurance?
LULU : No, only feathers; I'm a fan dancer.

The psychiatrist was having difficulty with his new client.

"I've told you from the start," he said, "I want you to be frank, and you don't seem able to be."

"That's the trouble," was the reply. "I don't know how to be frank, because I'm Percy."

LADY : My husband did as I asked and bought me a fur this Christmas.
NEIGHBOUR : That was nice of him, what kind was it?
LADY : A Christmas tree.

What was Sir Galahad's favourite game?
Knights and crosses.

LULU :Doesn't Elsie fancy herself in her new wig?

MARY : Rather. Every time she puts it on it goes to her head.

Why do we have a joint of meat for Sunday lunch?
Because Sunday is a day of Roast.

Tommy's aunt told him to let his little brother share part of the sweets she had brought. Later she asked the little boy if he had enjoyed them.

"Not much," he said.

"Why not?" said his aunt. "Didn't Tommy let you share part of them?"

"Oh yes," said the little brother. "He let me have the toffee papers!"

When is an actor like a boot black?
When he gives a polished performance.

FIRST ZANY: It's my twenty-first birthday next week.
SECOND ZANY: Oh . . . how old will you be?

PATIENT: So the X-rays reveal I'm quite normal?
DOCTOR: Indeed yes, both of your heads are perfectly O.K.

FIRST NEIGHBOUR: And how did your husband stand up to his operation?
SECOND NEIGHBOUR: He didn't. They said he had to lie down when they did it.

61

BIG DADDY'S CORNER

What's the difference between someone given permission, and the way Big Daddy treats his rivals?
One gets the O.K., the others get the K.O.

What's the difference between a poor wrestler and a short circuit?
One loses the fight. The other fuses the light.

What wrestling term do you get if you cross a good tuck-in with a well-known bird of prey?
A spread-eagle.

What wrestling term do you get if you cross a chief schoolmaster and a wine cask?
A head-butt.

What kind of hold would an Irish jockey use?
An Irish whip.

How would you describe Big Daddy's Wrestling Book?
A gripping story.

ROUND FIVE:

OUCH!

BANK MANAGER (To overdrawn customer): I'm afraid I still cannot pay your cheques, even if you do sign them "yours hopefully".

BEAUTY PARLOUR MANAGERESS: Remember you must be very tactful with certain clients.
NEW ASSISTANT: Don't worry, madam, I'm quite used to dealing with ugly customers.

PUPIL: How can I improve my piano playing professor?
PROFESSOR (wearily): Try playing with the lid down.

What did the lipstick say to the face powder?
Between us we can put a completely different complexion on things.

MAGISTRATE (To prisoner): You appear to have been very methodical in the way you carried out your burglaries.
PRISONER: Yes, your honour. I always believed in working to a strict crime-table.

What is the fish frier's favourite motto?
If at first you don't succeed, fry, fry and fry again.

TOM: Do you know anyone who's been on the telly?
TIM: Only my dog, before he was house trained.

FIRST SNAKE CHARMER: Why are you playing a guitar instead of a pipe, Hussan?
SECOND SNAKE CHARMER: I've got a new young snake, and he will only perform if I play pop-up music.

EXECUTIONER (To victim with head on block): Sorry about this, but they do say third time is lucky.

What did the bird say when he saw what was on the bird-table?
Crumbs!

DON: Did you know that Mac's living on borrowed time?
RON: Poor fellow, what's the matter with him?
DON: He still hasn't returned the watch I lent him six months ago.

Seeing a sad-looking motorist standing by a car with the bonnet up, a kindly lorry-driver stopped to ask if he could give a hand.

"It's not so much a hand I want," said the motorist. "I'm more in need of a toe (tow)."

FIRST MOTHER: Jimmy's going to take ten 'O' levels this term.

SECOND MOTHER: Is he going to have a coach?

FIRST MOTHER: No. It'll just be a new bike if he gets them.

The visitor was being shown round the dairy farm, and was very impressed by the way the cowman seemed to know each animal individually.

"How can you tell which cow is which" asked the visitor.

"Simple," said the cowman, "I've been milking them for years, and now I can easily tell one from the udder."

Why are opticians agreeable people?
Because they see eye-to-eye with their customers.

FIRST MUSIC CRITIC: After hearing Rottgut's Modern Symphony, did you find any passage with special appeal?

SECOND MUSIC CRITIC: Yes. The passage which led to the Exit from the hall.

What happened when the boy let off a firework in the loo?
It was a flash in the pan.

MOTHER: Poor Grandad's got a bad cold.
YOUNG SON: Oh... I wondered why his nose kept crying.

What did the prisoner say when he was told that he was going to be tortured on the rack?
Oh dear, it looks as though I'm in for a long stretch.

What happened when the thief stole a trayful of watches?
He took a lot of time in doing it.

BARBER (To rapidly balding customer): There is one consolation, sir. It won't be long before no-one will be able to harm a hair of your head.

PSYCHIATRIST: What seems to be the trouble?
CLIENT: I keep thinking that I'm a ghost.
PSYCHIATRIST: I wondered why you walked into my room when the door was still shut.

Why are draughtsmen very discreet?
Because they know where to draw the line.

ERNIE: My dentist comes from abroad.
BERNIE: Does that mean he's of foreign extraction?

HOUSEWIFE: My husband gave me a lot of early flowers for my birthday.

NEIGHBOUR: What flowers were they?

HOUSEWIFE: I'm not sure. I haven't put the seeds in yet.

Mrs. Smith was getting very fat, and so she went to the doctor to find out what to do about it.

"Mrs. Smith," he warned. "You must watch very carefully what you eat."

"Oh I do, doctor," she said, "and I never miss a mouthful."

PATIENT: I feel properly run down, doctor.

DOCTOR: Can you describe your symptoms?

PATIENT: Yes, there are tyre marks all over my chest.

INFLATE!

NEWS ITEM: At the village concert, Mr. Jones, the dairy farmer, did one of his comic churns.

CANNIBAL WIFE: I'm boiling the rival chief's head for supper tonight.
CANNIBAL HUSBAND: Good. I shall enjoy picking his brains.

FOR SALE: Two mathematical rabbits. Able to multiply quickly.

UNCLE: At your new school do you find anything particularly hard to take in?
NEPHEW: Only the school dinners.

RESTAURANT MANAGER (To job applicant): Have you had much experience of waiting?
JOB APPLICANT: Oh yes, sir. I've been travelling by bus for years.

FIRST MOTORIST: How did you get that dent in your car?
SECOND MOTORIST: Oh, just an acci-dent.

Why is a pony compared with a horse like a halfpenny?
Because it's a smaller mount (small amount).

Attending the local hospital is an eight foot tall patient. He is one of the hospital's longest sufferers.

What ant eats fish?
The cormorant.

What is a soldier ant?
A combat-ant.

DID YOU HEAR THE STORY OF:

The blunt pencil . . . (There was no point to it.)

The empty box . . . (There was nothing in it.)

The man who changed his address . . . (It was a moving tale.)

The judge who sat for forty years . . . (It was full of long sentences.)

The coach full of elderly shoemakers . . . (It was a load of old cobblers.)

The chinese sailing ship . . . (It was absolute junk.)

The umbrella . . . (It was a put-up job.)

What happened when the charlady's husband came home late one night?
She wiped the floor with him.

Where was the favourite meeting place for King Arthur's men?
The (k)night club.

What was the most difficult thing for a knight in armour to do?
Scratch himself.

MAGGIE: Whatever's the matter with your arm?

AGGIE: I asked my friend what he called his Alsatian.

MAGGIE: So what?

AGGIE: He said his name was "Caesar" . . . and so he did.

What sort of tiles can't be stuck on a wall?
Reptiles.

ZANY JUDGE: The sentence that I give to you, is six months you will have to do.

PRISONER: That's a funny sort of sentence.

ZANY JUDGE: No it isn't. It's what's called poetic justice.

FIRST ZANY: Next week I'm going to Honolulu.

SECOND ZANY: Will you fly?

FIRST ZANY: No, I'm going by aeroplane.

What roads are dangerous to drive on?
Slip roads.

What happened when the undertaker retired?
He went and buried himself in the country.

FIRST LOONY: I'm going to Piccadilly tomorrow.

SECOND LOONY: Oh goody. . . while you're there, will you pick me one?

When Mr. Jones came home from the office he asked his wife what she had been doing.

"Nothing much, dear," said Mrs. Jones. "Just window-shopping."

"That was a nice cheap day then," said Mr. Jones.

"Not exactly, dear," replied his wife. "When I said window-shopping I meant that I'd arranged for the house to be double-glazed."

Silly Sam decided to buy a wig. "I'd like one," he said, "with a large hole in the middle."

"But," said the wig-maker, "people will see that you're bald."

"Yes," said Silly Sam. "If people see I'm bald they won't think that I'm wearing a wig!"

FIRST SINGER: What is the highest note you can get when you sing?

SECOND SINGER: Sometimes I get a ten pound note, but usually it's a fiver.

FIRST CLUB MEMBER: I hear poor old Carruthers finished up as a cannibal's dinner.

SECOND CLUB MEMBER: Oh? Reminds me we went to the same school.

FIRST CLUB MEMBER: How interesting ... what was that?

SECOND CLUB MEMBER: Eton.

CUSTOMER: Have you smoked salmon, waiter?

WAITER: No, sir, never. I only smoke filter tips.

TEACHER: In Iran, what is the Ayatollah's deputy called?
BOY: The lower tollah, miss.

Fred was just back from the United States after doing a tour of various cities.

"Amongst the different places you went to did you make Chicago?" asked his friend.

"Sure," replied Fred. "Every time I pressed the starter it went."

What kind of cat swims under water?
An octo-pus(s)

BOB: I would have been top of the class list except for one thing.

CHARLIE: What was that?
BOB: The list would have had to have been upside-down.

Why is a savings account like a bed?
Because with both you get interest (In to rest).

PATIENT: After hearing what you said I want a second opinion.
DOCTOR: Certainly. After my first opinion my second one is just the same – there's nothing wrong with you.

ADVERT IN PET SHOP: Alligator for sale. Would exchange for wooden leg.

BIG DADDY'S CORNER

What's Big Daddy's favourite television programme?
"It's A Knock-out".

What's his favourite shell-fish?
Boston crab.

What sort of titled person would a wrestler meet with if he got knocked out?
The Count.

What part of a cargo ship is like a wrestling grip?
The hold.

Why is Big Daddy like a good artist?
Because he knows how to draw the crowds.

PERCY: Wrestlers remind me of jewellers.
JAMES: Why?
PERCY: Because they both know a lot about rings.

ROUND SIX:
FREE FOR ALL

"I saw old Jock go by in a Daimler this morning", said one Scotsman to another.

"Old Jock in a Daimler!" said his friend. "He was doing himself well. Did he see you?"

"A dinna think so," replied the first Scotsman. "It was his funeral."

House fly to bluebottle: I've simply got to fly, but I'll give you a buzz later.

FAT CUSTOMER: Is there anything special you would recommend, waiter?
WAITER: For you, sir, I would recommend slimming pills.

Why is a boxer like a hole in a flat tyre?
Because they are both punctures (punchers).

OLD LADY (To grocer): My cat's too old to catch mice now. I'll have to buy him some tinned food.
GROCER: What would you like, madam?
OLD LADY: Well, he'd better have tinned mice, I suppose.

FIRST WOMAN: We live on a house-boat.

SECOND WOMAN: Any special reason?

FIRST WOMAN: Yes, it's so handy. When I run short of money I just go to the bank.

FIRST PARTY GUEST: That man over there's got a wonderful figure.

SECOND PARTY GUEST: But he's short and fat — what's wonderful about that?

FIRST PARTY GUEST: It's the one he's got in the bank ... he's a millionaire.

FAY: Why does Pete always walk around with his mouth open?

MAY: Because he's lazy, and it saves him having to open it when he yawns.

FIRST CANNIBAL: The chief's new girlfriend looks a real dish.

SECOND CANNIBAL: Oh good; we'll have her tonight for supper.

CLIVE: How about you and I spending the weekend at a nudist camp?

HENRY: No fear, the bare thought's enough to put me off.

Did you hear about the Scottish motorist who was so polite that every time he met a lady friend, he got out of the car and raised his bonnet?

What was said to Emilion when he did someone a good turn?
Thanks Emilion. (Thanks a million).

What did Lady Hamilton say to Nelson?
You're the one-eye care for.

GARAGE MANAGER: Will you blow up this customer's tyres, Paddy?
PADDY: Sure, boss... where's the dynamite?

How did Aladdin get a living?
He managed to rub along with a lamp.

BESSIE: George has a very clear head.
JESSIE: You're right — he's got absolutely nothing in it.

What sort of people become nudists?
Those who like to see a lot of each other.

MAGISTRATE: What did the accused say when told he would be charged with shoplifting?
POLICEMAN: As the shop said it was a stock-taking sale, he thought he'd help by taking some.

Pat was sent on an errand, and was late coming back. His wife angrily asked him for an explanation.

"It was like this," he said. "In the shop, by the door, was a notice: WILL CUSTOMERS PLEASE MIND THE STEP – and I had to wait ten minutes before I could find another customer to take my place and mind it."

FRIEND: What are your favourite roles?
ACTOR: Hamlet, Othello, cheese and ham.

1ST MOTH: That new moth is terribly pernickety, isn't she?
2ND MOTH: Yes, I've noticed it too. She picks holes in everything.

WIFE: So you've had a very busy day, dear. Many accidents?
BREAKDOWN TRUCK DRIVER: Yes... a bumper number.

KNOCK KNOCK!
Who's there?

Ifor.
Ifor who?
I forgot the key.

Warner
Warner who?
Warner lift? My car's outside.

Obadiah
Obadiah who?
Obadhaih've rung twice already and got no answer.

Tina
Tina who?
Tina baked beans.

Fiona
Fiona who?
Fiona of the house. I've come for the rent.

Jeff
Jeff who?
Jeff in one ear – speak up!

Luke
Luke who?
Luke snappy and open this door!

Ezra
Ezra who?
Ezra doctor in the house?

Ike
Ike who?
Ike can't tell you.

Juno
Juno who?
I've no idea.

Adair
Adair who?
Adair once. Now I'm bald.

Wayne
Wayne who?
Wayne is coming down; I want my umbrella.

Chester
Chester who?
Chester minute! Don't you know who I am?

Anita
Anita who?
Anita borrow a pint of milk!

William
William who?
William make haste – it's freezing out here!

Francis
Francis who?
France is on the other side of the Channel.

Carmen
Carmen who?
Carmen see for yourself.

A safe cracking thief called McBride,
Once blew a safe door open wide.
When the dust cleared away,
He was filled with dismay,
For he found there was nothing inside.

The reason she smiled (Mona Lisa),
Was seeing the Tower of Pisa.
They didn't quite mean
To make the thing lean,
But they built it that way just to please 'er.

When accepting a young man at Kew,
A maiden said, "Yes, I'll be true.
"But you must understand
"Since you've asked for my hand
"That the rest of me goes with it too!"

Newton heard a sort of plonk –
An apple fell upon his conk;
Discovered gravitation law
It shook old Isaac to the core.

The bomb he set went off too soon,
And here his story ceases.
The bits they found are buried here –
So thus he Rests in Pieces.

An executive lady called Claire,
Would never put comb to her hair;
One day at a meeting,
She heard a tweet-tweeting
And found two small birds nesting there.

A steeple-chase jockey called Ron
A most obstinate mare sat upon.
When half round the course,
"That's enough," said the horse,
And she stopped while her rider went on.

Llewelly Peter James Maguire
Touched a live electric wire;
Back on his heels it sent him rocking –
His language (like the wire) was shocking.

The baker's daughter, Maisie Jones,
Had lots and lots of fun,
For every time she did her hair,
She put it in a bun.

BIG DADDY'S CORNER

What does Big Daddy's famous belly-butt prove?
That he has plenty of stomach for a fight.

When Big Daddy stops at the traffic lights, what can
they remind him of?
Unfair fighters, because they make him see red.

What do some wrestlers like to train on?
Bangers and smash!

What does Big Daddy think of his many supporters?
Absolutely FANtastic.

Why does Big Daddy find shining silk relaxing to wear?
Because it is satin (sat in)!

Why is Big Daddy famous?
Because he always makes BIG news.

ROUND SEVEN:
RIB-CRACKERS

What makes people shy?
Coconuts.

CIRCUS MANAGER: We've got to find someone t
replace the sword swallower.
BOSS: Why, what's wrong with him?
CIRCUS MANAGER: He wants to pack it in – he say
he's fed up to the hilt.

What does a million dollars do?
Makes a lot of cents (sense).

ST. PETER: None of our new arrivals get her
punctually!
ARCHANGEL GABRIEL: Not surprising, really. Aft
all, to get here they have to be "late".

NEW ANGEL TO CHERUB: You're lucky. I'm redu
dant here. I used to be a stoker.

What's the difference between a boy who hates washin
and a lazy man?
*One's all for water shirking. The other's all for shorte
working.*

PATIENT: The trouble is, I am afraid to travel by air.
PSYCHIATRIST: Then I can assure you that your fears are groundless.

Why are fishing stories nearly always difficult to believe?
Because there's generally a catch in them.

Why don't astronauts' jobs last very long?
Because when they start they are fired.

NEIGHBOUR: What are you getting your husband for Christmas?
WIFE: As he eats like a horse, I thought I'd give him a nose bag.

NEWS ITEM: Pelicans are very expensive to feed these days. Zoo-keepers are having to face very large bills.

Why are maggots like unreliable people?
Because they wriggle out of things.

Why did the milk-shake?
Because it was funny that whey.

Abe's brother took a note to school to say that his brother was unwell. The note only had four letters in it. What were they?
A.B.C.D. (Abe is seedy)

When is an Eskimo like a man with bare feet?
When he has snow shoes (no shoes) on.

What did Noah say when they reached the top of Mount Ararat?

'Ark! It's stopped raining.

What did Sherlock Holmes say to Doctor Watson in 1907?
I haven't a clue.

Why is water from a well like a will?
Because they are both drawn up.

PATIENT: I've got back trouble, doctor.
DOCTOR: There's no need to tell me. You're back every five minutes.

WIFE: The kitchen ought to be decorated.
HUSBAND: When I think of some of those meals you've cooked in it for me, so ought I.

Did you hear about the poultry farmer who mixed cocoa with the chickens' mash so they could lay chocolate easter eggs?

FRED: That new undertaker's very modern.
FREDA: Modern? What makes you think that?
FRED: He's renamed the funeral parlour and called it The Departure Lounge.

RICH ARAB: I'm very pleased to meet you, I'm an oil sheikh.
RICH DAIRY FARMER: How do you do, I'm a milk sheikh.

FIRST HEN: What do you think of the new cockerel?
SECOND HEN: I don't know about you, but I think his temper's absolutely fowl.

Absent Minded professor (at party): I remember your name, but I'm afraid I've forgotten your face.

What are the busiest hands in the whole world?
The hour and minute hands, because they work round the clock.

1ST OCTOPUS: I don't know what to buy my hubby for Christmas!
2ND OCTOPUS: Do the same as I did for mine, and get him four pairs of gloves.

Why is a lightning artist like a gunman?
Because they are both quick on the draw.

The undertaker had a request for a coffin six feet wide six feet long and six inches tall. "Why do you want one like that?" he asked. The reply came: "It's for a man who got run over by a steam-roller."

PAUL: Did you know that Jock was a trained singer?
SAUL: Could be — he can certainly hang on to a note for a long time.

What is someone who is mad about money?
A dough-nut.

MAC: Jock's very canny the way he uses his telephone.
SANDY: Why, what does he do?
MAC: He only uses it for long distance calls. For local ones he uses a megaphone.

What would a match between a boxer and a Japanese fighter resemble?
A Punch and Judo show.

JIM: My wife struck it rich the other day
TIM: Did she win the pools?
JIM: No. She drove the car into the High Street bank.

What is an American ant?
The wife of an American Uncle.

Why are horses used to draw carts?
Big-horse they are. (Because they are.)

Did you hear about the girl who thought a potting shed was an indoor rifle range?

TEACHER: What are doubloons?
BOY: Daft twins.

FRAN: What do you think of Jessie now she's put on such a lot of weight?
JAN: I think she looks absolutely swell.

What is the simplest way to increase the size of your bank balance?
Look at it through a magnifying glass.

What's the difference between a greedy boy and a toaster?
One takes the most. The other makes the toast.

FORTUNE-TELLER: I'm glad to say that you are going to come into a lot of money.
CUSTOMER: Splendid! When I do, I'll be able to pay you.

Why are tattooists scheming people?
Because they have designs on others.

What happened to the cat after he'd drunk a saucerful of milk.
He was purr-fectly satisfied.

Why are Manx cats good at keeping secrets?
Because they are not tale (tail) bearers.

What did Hamlet say when he found he was putting on weight?
Tubby or not tubby . . . that is the question!

HARRY: When you went on holiday did you enjoy the change?

LARRY: Everything was so expensive I never got any.

Why do cowboys ride bucking broncos?
For kicks.

How do undertakers calculate the cost of a funeral?
By dead reckoning.

What describes a yearning for food?
Nosh-talgia.

Why is a banana skin like a dressing gown?
Because it is easy to slip on.

What did the lumberjack do just before Christmas?
He went on a chopping spree.

BIG DADDY'S CORNER

Why is Big Daddy bound to be a striking success?
Because he is a match for anybody.

Why does Big Daddy's height make him a difficult wrestler to beat?
Because trying to get the better of him is a very tall order.

What did the wrestler say when Big Daddy yanked him right across the ring?
I feel a proper jerk!

What do you get if you cross Big Daddy's topper with a pop group?
A hat band.

When do Big Daddy's opponents look like fried fish?
When they are battered.

Why does Big Daddy always keep his "cool"?
Because he has lots of good fans around him.

What famous book does Big Daddy remind you of?
"The Lord of the Rings".

109

ROUND EIGHT:
KNOCK-OUTS

What does an ant become when it's angry?
A milit-ant.

CUSTOMER (phoning): May I have a table for dinner tonight?

WITTY WAITER : A table? Yes sir ... How would you like it — roast, boiled or fried?

JUDGE (After sentencing prisoner): Have you anything to say?

PRISONER : Yes, your honour. Since I'm being clapped in jail may I ask when the applause will begin?

What's the difference between someone rushing to the railway station and an athlete preparing for a race?
One races for the train. The other trains for the race.

When is an envelope like a snooty person?
When it's stuck up.

What sort of meat did Dracular particularly hate?
Steak (stake).

What did the trampoline performer say?
Life has its ups and downs, but I always bounce back.

DOCTOR: From what you tell me, you seem to have vertigo.

PATIENT: Not really, doctor. I only live in the next street from here.

What does a taxi driver do?
Makes a fare living.

What sort of noise does a horse make going backwards?
Cloppity clip, cloppity clip.

What's the difference between a square peg in a round hole, and three pounds of lard?
One's a fat lot of good, the other's a good lot of fat.

What monkey is like a flower?
A chimp-pansy (chimpanzee).

What did the caterpillar say to his young girl friend?
Luverly grub.

What is the undertaker's most unfavourite motto?
Never say die.

What sort of bird starts on two legs and finishes up on four?
A turkey, because it ends up on the table.

Mr. and Mrs. Brown had a parrot for over thirty years. Unfortunately it never spoke a word, but then Mrs. Brown died, and the parrot suddenly addressed Mr. Brown. "I'm very sorry about your wife," it said.

"Good heavens!" exclaimed Mr. Brown. "I didn't think you could talk!"

"Well," said the parrot. "Today is the first chance I've ever had to get a word in edgeways."

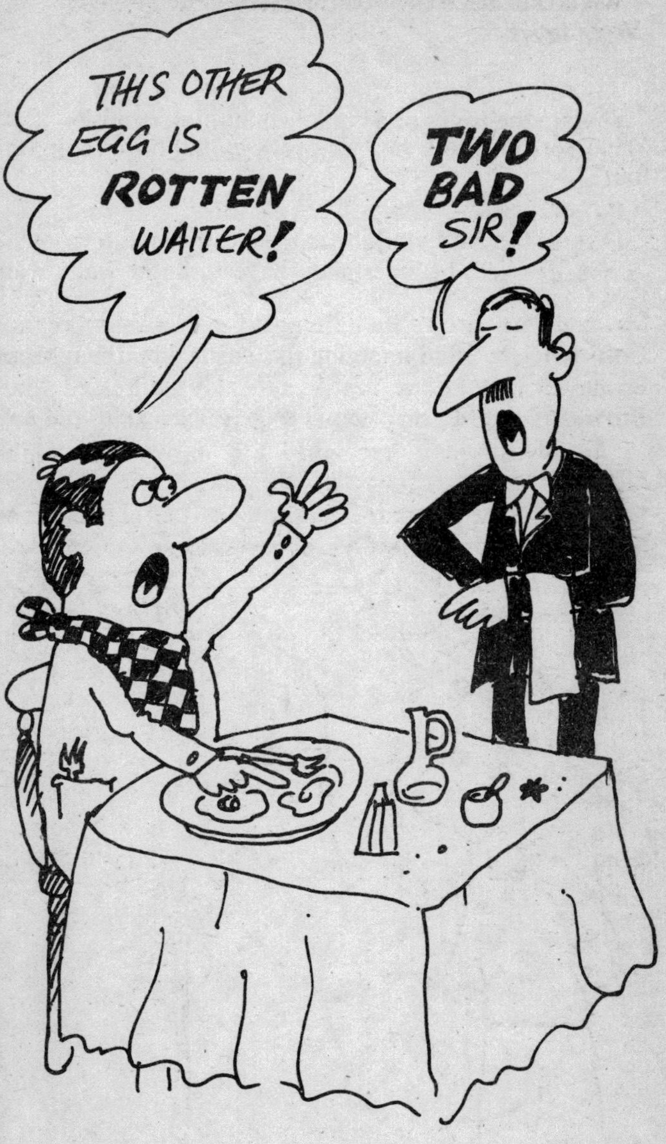
THIS OTHER EGG IS ROTTEN WAITER!
TWO BAD SIR!

What do dentists wear on their feet?
Gum-boots.

Why are the pages of a book like faithful friends?
Because they are bound to stick together.

MAISIE: Gerald's working in the electricity showroom.
DAISIE: Well, he'll certainly have to know watts watt.

1ST GHOST: I find haunting this castle a real drag these
days.
2ND GHOST: Me too. I don't seem to be able to put any
life into it.

1ST MUM: My Eddie will have to start thinking about getting a job.
2ND MUM: Has he any particular leaning for anything?
1ST MUM: At the moment it's only on walls and lamp posts.

Does your dog moult?
Only when his hair comes out.

What is Dracula's favourite slogan?
Please give blood generously.

What happened when the two kangaroos got married?
It was a very hoppy occasion.

What's the difference between sitting on a wasp and a cowpuncher?
One stings the rear, the other rings the steer.

What did the French think of the English bowmen at the Battle of Agincourt?
That they were an arrow-minded lot (a narrow-minded lot).

What happened when the two cannibal tribes fought one another?
The side that won made mince-meat of the other.

How do Eskimos stop their mouths from freezing?
They grit their teeth.

What did the American nudist say to the cop?
You ain't got nothing on me!

Why is it nice to drink instant coffee?
Because it leaves no grounds for complaint.

Why is a bargain like a farewell?
Because they are both good-byes (good buys).

What did the ant say to the elephant?
You look simply great.

HETTY: Mabel's got a new job. She's restoring antiques.
BETTY: Where does she work?
HETTY: In a beauty treatment parlour.

What are coronation teeth?
Ones that have been crowned.

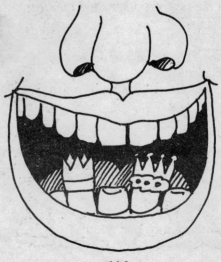

What sort of ship is like a crying baby?
A whaler (wailer).

MRS. BROWN: My son George never seems to be able to keep a girl for long.
MRS. JONES: Well, you know the old saying. A rolling stone gathers no miss.

Why is it always nice to have dinner.
Because it is plate-time (play time).

FIRST AUSTRALIAN: I see that boomerang throwing is getting very popular again.
SECOND AUSTRALIAN: Sure – it's making a real comeback.

Why is it nice being a baby?
Because it is a nappy time.

VERY FAT PERSON: When I got on the scales this morning I registered eight stone.
FRIEND: Your scales can't be very accurate.
VERY FAT PERSON : Yes they are. All I had to allow for was that the needle had already gone round once.

Why didn't George Washington tell a lie when he chopped the tree down?
Because he was an honest feller.

Did you hear about the witch's identical twins?
You couldn't tell which was which...

What's the difference between a recorder and a chiropodist?
One tapes the shows. The other shapes the toes.

What's the difference between a jousting knight and someone who misses an opportunity?
One chooses his lance. The other loses his chance.

CUSTOMER: I'll have some champagne, and make sure you bring it in an ice bucket.
NEW WAITER: That's a bit unusual, sir. Most customers like it in a nice glass.

Why did the daft man like to be by himself.
Because he preferred to be a loon.

What kind of boat is like a tailor?
A cutter.

Why do smartly-dressed men get good jobs?
Because they are well suited.

What happened when the parachutist fell in the sea?
It was just a drop in the ocean.

BOSS: Have you considered early retirement?
EMPLOYEE: Yes indeed, sir. I always go to bed at 9.30.

What happened when the disc jockey dropped a record?
It was a case of a slipped disc.

If milk comes from a cow, where does wine come from?
A wine-ocerous.

What's the difference between a gymnast and a tobogganist?
One slides down the rope. The other rides down the slope.

What's the difference between Blackpool and an electric drill?
One's a "pool" that's got the Tower. The other's a tool that's got the power.

What is a road hog?
A pig-headed driver.

JEAN: Lucy is a very self-possessed person, isn't she?
JOAN: Quite. No one else would own her.

ENQUIRER: Do you think your lectures on how to lose weight will be popular?
LECTURER: In view of the subject, I am bound to get a large audience.

NEWS ITEM: Mr. Jones was summonsed by the court for allowing his dog to bite the postman's leg. He was ordered to keep the peace (piece).

1ST RAMBLER: Where do you hike most?
2ND RAMBLER: In my feet. These boots are too tight.

1ST WOMAN: Is your husband a coarse fisherman?
2ND WOMAN: Only if he doesn't catch anything.

What happened when the fat man got run over by a steam roller?
It proved he had plenty of guts.

What happened to the kleptomaniac's daughter?
She took after her mother.

FIRST MOTORIST: I think the breathalyser is a bad thing for the country.
SECOND MOTORIST: Why?
FIRST MOTORIST: Because when you blow into it it causes inflation.

EVE: I'm fed up with you, Adam. I'm leaving!
ADAM: O.K. Where are you going? I know you can't g‹
back to Mother.

Why are Londonders nice people?
Because they are capital folk.

The impatient customer approached the shop-assistan‹
and complained that no one appeared to be serving a‹
his counter.

"I'm sorry, sir," said the shop-assistant, "but I'm
afraid we're very short-staffed."

"In that case," said the customer, "why don't you
employ taller ones so that they can be seen more
easily?"

MAY I HELP YOU SIR?

Why is putting a shoe on like making a mistake?
Because when you do you put your foot in it.

GOSSIP COLUMN ITEM: Count Dracula has denied that he is to marry the Viscountess Vampire. They remain just good fiends.

Who were the first people to write with pens?
The Incas (Inkers).

What's the difference between a good-natured dog and a bad scholar?
One rarely bites, the other barely writes.

What's the difference between someone who deals with pots and pans and someone who deals with plots and plans?
An 'L' of a difference.

NEWS ITEM: Undertakers will stage an annual exhibition at Wembley. It will be known as "The Hearse of the Year Show".

REPORTER: And how did you learn to become such a good actor?
ACTOR: I did it in various stages.

What is a noisy soccer fan?
A foot-bawler.

THE AWFUL JOKE BOOK

compiled by Mary Danby

The best of the worst! Here is a great new
collection of ghastly gags, hideous howlers,
riotous riddles and witty wisecracks –
illustrated with scores of hilarious cartoons.
You'll drive your family and friends
round the bend! Here are a couple of
examples . . .

What is the main ingredient in dog biscuits?
Collie flour.

NEW COWHAND: What is the name of this ranch?
RANCHER: The Lazy G Triple Diamond Circle S
    Bar Z.
NEW COWHAND: How many head of cattle are there?
RANCHER: Not many. Only a few of them survive the
    branding.

Armada

TOP OF THE POPS QUIZ

Peter Eldin

Test your knowledge of the fabulous world of pop
with 100 exciting quizzes and puzzles about all
today's – and yesterday's – most popular stars.

Featuring the presenters of television's favourite pop
programme – Kid Jensen, David Lee Travis,
Peter Powell, Simon Bates and Mike Read – *Top of
the Pops Quiz* is certain to head straight for the
top of the charts.

Armada

CAPTAIN ARMADA

has a whole shipload of exciting books for you

Here are just some of the best-selling titles that Armada has to offer:

- ⊐ **The Mystery of the Magic Circle** Alfred Hitchcock 80p
- ⊐ **Smuggler** (TV Tie-in) Richard Carpenter 85p
- ⊐ **Cassidy in Danger** Diana Pullein-Thompson 80p
- ⊐ **Garden Fun** Roger Smith 75p
- ⊐ **The Flying Saucer Mystery** Carolyn Keene 80p
- ⊐ **The Secret Agent's Handbook** Peter Eldin 80p
- ⊐ **The Hardy Boys Survival Handbook** Franklin W. Dixon 85p
- ⊐ **12th Armada Crossword Book** Robert Newton 80p
- ⊐ **The Popeye Storybook** (Film Tie-in) £1.95
- ⊐ **Big Daddy's Joke Book** 85p

Armadas are available in bookshops and newsagents, but can also be ordered by post.

HOW TO ORDER
ARMADA BOOKS, Cash Sales Dept., GPO Box 29, Douglas, Isle of Man, British Isles. Please send purchase price of book plus postage, as follows:—

> 1—4 Books .... 10p per copy
> 5 Books or more .... no further charge
> 25 Books sent post free within U.K.

Overseas Customers: 12p per copy

NAME (Block letters)

ADDRESS